JOHN JAY

A Life From Beginning to End

Copyright © 2018 by Hourly History.

Table of Contents

Introduction

The Forgotten Founding Father

His likeness has not been carved into the rock of Mount Rushmore, where iconic Founding Fathers George Washington and Thomas Jefferson dominate the landscape along with later presidents Abraham Lincoln and Teddy Roosevelt; John Jay never won the White House. His features don't grace American currency, unlike those of Alexander Hamilton whose right to be honored on the ten-dollar bill was upheld with a bit of help from a Broadway musical. Unlike John Adams, John Jay was not celebrated in an award-winning television miniseries, although Adams praised Jay for his work in negotiating the Treaty of Paris which ended the American Revolution. John Jay was integral to the scaffolding that built 13 independent and quarrelsome colonies into the United States, but it seems as though he has disappeared from the annals of his country's record.

The Central Intelligence Agency, however, did not forget him for his work as a spymaster during the war against Great Britain that established the colonies as a free nation. When the CIA opened its Liaison Conference Center in 1997, the three meeting rooms were named for three separate areas of espionage. George Washington and Benjamin Franklin were recognized for their work in foreign intelligence and covert action. The third meeting room was named in honor of John Jay for his work in counterintelligence during the American Revolution.

Even in these days of heightened awareness of other nations and their efforts to undermine American security, few people realize that John Jay was a spymaster in New York, sending agents on missions to determine what plots were afoot among the British and their Loyalist allies in New York. There's irony in the fact that the exploits of the Father of American Counterintelligence have so effectively, albeit unintentionally, been concealed.

Who is this man who was remembered more by the CIA than by historians devoted to the subject of American history? John Jay was the son of a successful merchant; French Huguenot origins on his father's side and Dutch ancestry from his mother's side made him the typical New World hybrid where a new ethnic identity was being forged from the different bloodlines of Europe. He was a cautious man who was not immediately convinced that independence was the desired goal as the colonies began to regard their British ties as a yoke of servitude. But after he was converted to the Patriot cause, he was committed to its success.

He served his country as a delegate to the Continental Congress, then was sent abroad, first to Spain to seek recognition and a loan, and then to France, where he was one of the negotiators for the Treaty of Paris to bring the war against Great Britain to an official end. Recognizing the inherent weaknesses of the Articles of Confederation which had governed the nation in its earliest days, Jay was a supporter of the Constitution and, along with Alexander Hamilton and James Madison, one of the authors of the Federalist Papers. He served the government as the Secretary of Foreign Affairs and Secretary of State, and then became the first Chief Justice of the Supreme Court.

His role as the negotiator of what became known as Jay's Treaty may have cost him any hopes of becoming president. The Treaty was unpopular, even though it was pragmatic in avoiding a second war with Great Britain before the country was strong enough to fight it.

John Jay had a resume that matched those of his fellow Founding Fathers. Why, then, is he an afterthought in the historical accounts? Historian Walter Stahr, his biographer, believes that the reason is Jay himself. "Unlike John Adams, who spent a lot of time defending his place in history, Jay does not spend a lot of time on that. He answers letters as they arrive, but doesn't seek out writing engagements. The War of 1812 is very worrisome because he devoted a lot of his time to avoiding that. And he worried about the emerging tensions between North and South. In the end, he's more worried about America than he is about John Jay."

It is time that this forgotten Founding Father is found.

Chapter One

The Jays of New York

"It has often given my pleasure to observe, that independent America was not composed of detached and distant territories, but that one connected fertile, wide-spreading country was the portion of our western sons of liberty. Providence has in a particular manner blessed it with a variety of soils and productions, and watered it with innumerable streams, for the delight and accommodation of its inhabitants. A succession of navigable waters form a kind of chain round its borders, as if to bind them together; while the most noble rivers in the world, running at convenient distances, present them with highways for the easy communication of friendly aids, and the mutual transportation of their various ties."

—John Jay

The colony of New York was not, to be sure, as refined or elegant as that of the European countries where centuries of protocol had carved a rigid sense of class and order into society. New York had begun its existence as a Dutch colony known as New Amsterdam at a time when the Spanish, French, English, and Dutch had all sought to imprint their mastery upon the raw new land on the other side of the Atlantic Ocean. The Manhattan tribe had sold the land to the Dutch in 1626; at least that was how the Dutch viewed the transaction, which cost them a mere $24 worth of trinkets. But the Manhattan view of property did not mesh with the Western view, and the Indians and the Dutch eventually expressed their dissatisfaction with the deal in martial terms. In 1641, war broke out between the Dutch colonists and the Manhattan tribe, leading to the death of over 1,000 settlers and native Americans.

In 1664, New Amsterdam became New York as Governor Peter Stuyvesant surrendered the Dutch colony to the English and the city was renamed New York in honor of the English Duke of York.

Regardless of these conflicts and squabbles, the colony was an inviting one for people in Europe who were weary of the endless wars, the lack of opportunity, the rigid social structure, and the religious strife. For those people, the freedom offered in a new land was worth the danger, and they crossed the ocean in search of a way of life in which their own merit, not the pedigree of ancestors, would be the means by which they would advance.

Where the Dutch, English, French, and Spanish were foes in Europe, they would become neighbors and fellow citizens in the colonies, intermarrying with arrivals from other nations to create a new ethnic identity in the land that would eventually become the United States of America.

One of those families was the Jays. The Jays of New York traced their ancestry back to the French Huguenots who had fled France in search of safety and religious freedom after the 1685 revocation of the Edict of Nantes that took away the rights of Protestants and confiscated their property. Augustus Jay and his sister left France for Virginia and from there went to New York. It was a good move, as Augustus' business acumen led him to a thriving career as a merchant. The family business did well and Augustus' son Peter, born in 1704, continued to build upon that solid foundation by trading in commodities such as fur, wheat, and timber, products which were readily produced in the resource-rich agricultural New World colony.

In 1728, Peter Jay married a New Yorker, Mary Van Cortlandt, whose line came through the Dutch settlers of the colony. The Jay-Van Cortlandt connection must have had the blessings of the family because Frederick Van Cortlandt, Mary's brother, also married into the Jay family.

Mary's father, Jacobus Van Cortlandt, had been born in 1658 and had a flourishing political career, serving twice as the mayor of New York City, as well as on the New York Assembly. Jacobus also held other offices, both judicial and military; this political trait would show up in his grandson, John, who would take politics to a level which the Van Cortlandts could not have envisioned.

Peter and Mary Jay had ten children; seven survived into adulthood. Of the seven, several were afflicted with mental handicaps. When a smallpox epidemic struck and blinded two of the children, the family moved to Rye, New York. By then, Peter Jay had retired from his business. Son John was born on December 23, 1745, the sixth of the seven children who survived into adulthood, three months before the move out of Manhattan.

For the next eight years, John Jay remained in Rye, where he was taught by his mother. He then went to New Rochelle, where he studied under an Anglican clergyman, Pierre Stoupe, for three years before returning home to Rye and taking instruction with his mother and George Murray.

When he was 14, Jay entered King's College, today Columbia University. He and Robert Livingston, whose father was a member of New York's upper class, became friends. Jay's friendships and contacts during his years at King's College would lead to a deeper interest in politics at a time when the political situation with Europe was becoming increasingly complicated.

New York was a British colony, and Great Britain had just fought a war with France. The French and Indian War, also known as the Seven Years' War, was fought on the American frontier. Loyalties were beyond dispute; the colonials and the British fought together against the French. But the Seven Years' War, which was won by the British, stemmed from the continental conflicts across the ocean and the hunger for the lands beyond the Mississippi on the American continent. The end of the war would not solve the fissures which opened up as the colonists would begin to question the constraints of their ties to the mother country.

After graduating in 1764 with high honors, Jay became a clerk in the law office of Benjamin Kissam. It was an advantageous position, as Kissam was much sought after as an instructor in the law during an era when members of the legal profession learned their craft by studying under an established lawyer. Jay was admitted to the New York bar in 1768, working as a lawyer along with his King's College friend, Robert Livingston, and, in 1771, setting up his own law office. He also became involved in local government matters, serving as the clerk for the New York-New Jersey Boundary Commissions, advancing in his professional career.

Jay continued his connections to the New York elite and in April 1774, when he was 28 years old, he married the 17-year-old daughter of the governor of New Jersey, Sarah Livingston, a union that would prove beneficial in the advancement of Jay's political fortunes. As the American colonies matured, political alliances were beginning to be forged through marital ties.

Politics was beginning to dominate the conversation of the New York leadership, particularly after Great Britain passed what to the colonists became known as the Intolerable Acts. The situation in Massachusetts, where political action had taken a radical turn after local agitators threw 342 chests of tea into Boston Harbor rather than pay an unpopular tax, led to the closing of the port.

Until the cost of the lost tea was compensated, the Crown decreed that the British were in charge. General Gage, who was the British commander of the forces in North America, was named governor. Town meetings were forbidden. British officers were authorized to house soldiers in the homes of private citizens. At this time, many colonial leaders were inclined to be cautious; the revolutionary fervor which seemed to have taken over the minds of Bostonians had not swept into the other colonies.

Still, there was cause for alarm. If the British could take away the rights of Bostonians, what was to prevent them from doing the same in the other colonies?

Chapter Two

The Continental Congress

"The Americans have tarred and feathered your subjects, plundered your merchants, burnt your ships, denied all obedience to your laws and authority; yet so clement and so long forbearing has our conduct been that it is incumbent on us now to take a different course. Whatever may be the consequences, we must risk something; if we do not, all is over."

—Prime Minister Lord North

The colony of New York was led by cautious men who were disinclined to hurry into conflict. When the Boston Committees of Correspondence sent a letter recommending that the colonies stop their trade with the British, New York merchants refused. But they did suggest that that the colonies needed to meet as a group to address the matter. The New York delegation wrote, "Upon these reasons we conclude that a congress of deputies from the colonies in general is of the utmost moment; that it ought to be assembled without delay, and some unanimous resolution formed in this fatal emergency, not only respecting your deplorable circumstances, but for the security of our common rights."

Recognizing that the passing of the Intolerable Acts required some kind of response and eager to forestall anything that resembled the Bostonian reaction, the conservative New York leadership named a committee to elect delegates to the Continental Congress. John Jay, the scion of an influential merchant family and the newlywed son-in-law of a New Jersey governor, was one of the delegates.

Twelve of the colonies sent delegates. Georgia, because of attacks from the Creek tribe, needed the help of the British military and did not participate. The mood of the delegates was not to break away from the mother country but rather to have their grievances heard by the government in London.

The First Continental Congress met in Philadelphia on September 5, 1774. At the age of 28, John Jay was the second-youngest member of the Congress. Despite his youth, he was not radical in his political leanings. His father had been a Whig and Jay followed in that path. He was opposed to breaking away from Great Britain and, like many of the Founding Fathers, had a great respect for the law and an equally great suspicion of mob rule. But he supported the rights of the colonies' citizens and was wary of British efforts to encroach upon the freedoms that the colonists felt they were entitled to receive.

As a delegate to the First Continental Congress, Jay joined others who wished to put the problems with Great Britain behind them and achieve a reconciliation which would bring the British and the colonials back in unity again. He helped to write the *Olive Branch Petition,* a document which aimed to avoid war between Great Britain and its colonies. The Second Continental Congress adopted the *Olive Branch Petition* on July 5, 1775.

The British may have found it difficult to believe the American protestations of loyalty considering that the following day saw the Second Continental Congress issue the *Declaration of the Causes and Necessity of Taking up Arms*. At any rate, Great Britain rejected the petition and, in August, declared its wayward colonies to be in a state of rebellion. King George III had refused to read the *Olive Branch Petition*, indicating that he was not disposed to reconciliation.

Jay retired from the First Continental Congress in 1776; by then, the issue of independence was in the forefront of the minds of many of the colonial leaders who, recognizing that the intransigent British would not relent, were actively seeking to break away from Great Britain. Jay, who returned home to New York, did not sign the Declaration of Independence and historians are not sure whether he wanted to do so or was not quite ready for that final act of separation.

Jay's return to his home colony saw continued involvement in political matters. As a member of the New York City Committee of Sixty, Jay tried to enforce the non-importation agreement that the First Continental Congress had passed.

Unfortunately, the actions of the British were not conducive to nurturing a spirit of reconciliation, and tensions began to escalate. In April 1775, bloodshed had already been spilled in Lexington and Concord,

Massachusetts as colonials and British troops traded fire. Matters seemed to worsen, and not only in Massachusetts.

The southern colony of Virginia, which was ruled by a royal governor, the Earl of Dunmore, ordered British marines to move the colony's gunpowder from where it was stored in Williamsburg to a ship belonging to the Royal Navy. The colonial legislature was alarmed, the militia was called up, and the governor, mindful of what had happened in Boston, fled Williamsburg with his family in June 1775 for the safety of a Royal Navy ship. Virginia began to experience the ramifications of the outpouring of patriotic spirit, and the Loyalists, also known as Tories, began to leave the city of Norfolk, where they had been in the majority.

The Whigs, or Patriots, remained in the city and amassed a military unit in case the British would attack. In December 1775, Governor Dunmore positioned four ships along the Norfolk waterfront and on Christmas Eve, the captain of one of the ships, the *Liverpool*, announced that he needed provisions and would prefer to purchase them and not take them by force. The message that he would use force if necessary was implicit. He also objected to the drilling and parading of the Whig troops along the waterfront. He suggested that it might be prudent for the women and children to leave Norfolk. January 1, 1776, saw the British firing on Norfolk, shelling the town and sending landing parties ashore to set fire to specific properties.

The citizens of other colonies watched this event unfold with alarm and many, Jay among them, were moved to support independence from Great Britain, switching his stance from that of a moderate to that of a Patriot. Like many other colonists who were moderates, the inspiration to seek separation from Great Britain resulted in the recognition of what a mighty power could do if it chose, even when it meant suppressing the rights of the citizens. War, John Jay decided, was inescapable.

The colonies realized that the move to independence affected how they conducted their business. Jay was as involved in the business of New York as he was in the development of the fledgling American nation. And his election to the Third New York Provincial Congress made him a participant in the drafting of New York's Constitution in 1777. The new political climate had a darker side as well, as citizens of New York who had once regarded themselves as British now parted ways and loyalties. The time for choosing had come: American or British.

It's easy to forget that the Founding Fathers, central though they were to the formation of a new nation which was as much a sociological experiment as a political enterprise, had duties to fulfill as leaders in their home states. This was the case for Jay as well, who on May 8, 1777, was elected Chief Justice of the New York Supreme Court of Judicature by the New York Provincial Congress. He would serve in this position for two years, a harbinger of the role he would play in later years when he would occupy the position of Chief Justice of the new nation's Supreme Court.

In 1778, Jay was once again elected to the Continental Congress. Later that year, his national duties interrupted his state assignments when he became the president of the Continental Congress. He was replacing Henry Laurens, with whom he had an adversarial relationship. The election for the assignment took place just three days after Jay became a delegate; four states voted for Laurens, and eight voted for Jay. The position was not of itself an influential one, as it was a ceremonial role. Jay served in this capacity from December 10, 1778, to September 28, 1779.

The war, which for so long had seemed to be a losing endeavor, began to take a different direction after the French chose to ally themselves with the new nation, sending troops, ships, and support. The American nation was greatly in need of an infusion of trained military assistance and funds. The war had not been going well. With the arrival of the French, including the Marquis de Lafayette, who became a great favorite of General Washington, the tide began to turn.

Chapter Three

The Father of American Counterintelligence

"I hasten this express to request you to order Captain Townsend's company of Rangers to repair immediately to the barn, situated on the west side of Butter-Hill, and there to secrete themselves until we arrive, which will be tomorrow evening, probably about eleven o'clock."

—Enoch Crosby

When the American Revolution began, loyalties which had hitherto been devoted to Great Britain became a matter of national significance. British sympathizers were viewed, not without justification, as spies or traitors. It's estimated that when the United States declared its separation from the British, only one-third of the nation was actually committed to American independence. One-third was indifferent, and another third regarded themselves as Loyalists, or Tories, so much so that there were more colonial soldiers opting to serve under the British flag than there were serving in the Continental army.

In the summer of 1776, John Jay was the chair of a committee investigating a Loyalist plot recruiting people to sabotage New York City targets in order to facilitate occupation by the British. Heading the conspiracy were William Tryon, the British royal governor of New York, and David Matthews, the mayor of New York City. Jay's investigation revealed these conspirators and their plot and also showed that the plan involved capturing or killing General George Washington. One of Washington's bodyguards, Thomas Hickey, was executed for his crime. The guilty governor took up residence on a British ship in New York Harbor, and Mayor Matthews was put in jail.

By autumn, British General Sir Henry Clinton was offering land and money to enlist Loyalists to join the British army or serve as spies in the area along the Hudson River, which was of strategic importance north of New York City. The New York State Committee and Commission for Detecting and Defeating Conspiracies was formed, and John Jay served as its first chairman.

During his term, he conducted many investigations which led to arrest and trial of suspects who were loyal to the British. He is known to have had at least ten agents to help conduct the investigations; his favorite was Elijah Hunter, who supervised a network of agents in the Fishkill area and would later work as a double agent in New York City. Enoch Crosby, another of Jay's agents, may have served as the model for the character of Harvey Birch in the novel *The Spy* by James Fennimore Cooper. Crosby also worked in the Fishkill area, where he joined Tory groups and learned about their activities in support of the British and then reported his findings to Jay.

In October 1777, Jay sent Crosby on a mission to a town on the western bank of the Hudson River where his agent would, as he always did, infiltrate the local Loyalist settings. Operating under the name of John Smith, Crosby was recruited into a military unit that a British officer was putting together. Within a week, Crosby sent a message to Jay, alerting him to send a company of Rangers the following day to a barn on the west side of Butter-Hill; a Loyalist unit of thirty men was scheduled to arrive around eleven o'clock.

The Rangers found the Loyalist unit as they had expected. In an attempt to hide, Crosby concealed himself in a haystack, but when the Rangers probed the haystack with bayonets, he surrendered. The leader of the Rangers was unaware that John Smith was actually a Patriot named Enoch Crosby. Crosby, along with the Loyalists, was taken to the home of John Jay and locked up. Jay was not there at the time, but a maid in his household recognized Crosby. She gave the men guarding him brandy laced with a sedative and Crosby made his escape.

Jay proved to be a success at running the network of spies, with approximately 500 cases investigated. To contain Loyalists who had been arrested by American forces, Jay established prison ships on the river. In May 1777, he proposed that civilian courts could be given the authority to handle treasons, insurrection, and the violation of oaths of allegiance because they would be more objective in their investigations and trials. Eventually, the military courts absorbed this task.

Jay took his spying seriously because he recognized that there would be times when the government had to conduct covert activities to maintain the security of the nation. He expanded upon this theory in *Federalist Paper Number 64*, writing, "There are cases where the most useful intelligence may be obtained, if the persons possessing it can be relieved from apprehensions of discovery. Those apprehensions will operate on those persons whether they are actuated by mercenary or friendly motives, and there doubtless are many of both descriptions, who would rely on the secrecy of the President, but who would not confide in that of the Senate, and still less in that of a large popular assembly. The convention has done well therefore in so disposing of the power of making treaties, that although the President must, in forming them, act by the advice and consent of the Senate, yet he will be able to manage the business of intelligence in such a manner as prudence may suggest."

Chapter Four

Negotiating the Treaty of Paris

"It having pleased the Divine Providence to dispose the hearts of the most serene and most potent Prince George the Third, by the grace of God, king of Great Britain, France, and Ireland . . . and of the United States of America, to forget all past misunderstandings and differences that have unhappily interrupted the good correspondence and friendship which they mutually wish to restore, and to establish such a beneficial and satisfactory intercourse, between the two countries upon the ground of reciprocal advantages and mutual convenience as may promote and secure to both perpetual peace and harmony. "

—Treaty of Paris

From state to nation to the international stage, John Jay continued to be entrusted with diplomatic responsibilities when on September 27, 1779, he was named minister to Spain with the goal of convincing Spain to recognize the United States as an independent nation free of British sovereignty. He was also sent to obtain financial assistance and to negotiate treaties to nurture the new country's trade. It was not enough just to win independence; the

United States needed to establish its economic independence as well. Freedom from Great Britain meant proving itself as a trading power among other nations rather than depending upon British markets for its products.

The assignment was challenging. The court of Spain would not recognize American independence; therefore it did not recognize Jay in his role as a minister of the United States. The Spanish had their own reasons for their stance which had nothing to do with their relations with Great Britain or their views on American independence. Spain worried that if they recognized American independence, their own colonies would seize upon the opportunity and seek freedom from Spain as the Americans had done with Great Britain. Historian Stacy Schiff observed that despite enduring financial and physical hardships in support of American independence, including "30 murderous months on the periphery of the Spanish court," Jay maintained his composure and his dignity.

The American Revolution was not an isolated conflict on a far-away continent. In truth, because of the tangled nature of European alliances and hostilities, it was a world war involving Great Britain, France, Spain, and the Netherlands. Then, on October 19, 1781, the British forces surrendered to the Americans, and the world turned upside down. The news of the British surrender reached London on November 25; King George III did not want to give up the fight, and Prime Minister Lord North resigned in March 1782. The British government and the American government would need to meet to agree to terms for a peace treaty to end the war.

On June 23, 1782, Jay arrived in France to negotiate the Treaty of Paris so that the American War of Independence would officially conclude. The aim of the treaty was to end the war which had occupied the former colonies and the British for close to a decade. As part of the process, the treaty would acknowledge American independence and recognize that the 13 former colonies were now a single entity consisting of free, independent states. The signing of the treaty would require Great Britain to conclude separate peace accords with each of the involved countries.

The war had proven to be a financial burden for the British. The prime minister who replaced Lord North died three months after taking office. King George III was not willing to surrender the rich and fertile territory that had added to Great Britain's influence, but the American negotiators recognized that they had the advantage in the proceedings.

Joining Jay in Paris were John Adams and Benjamin Franklin. The negotiating committee was originally intended to number five; however, Henry Laurens was captured by the British en route to France and was kept in the Tower of London until the war ended. After he was released, failing health prevented him from joining the negotiating committee. Thomas Jefferson, the fifth member of the committee, failed to leave the United States in sufficient time to participate in the negotiations.

The remaining three men would prove themselves up to the task.

The United States was to negotiate first with the British and then with the French in order to conclude the treaty. In July 1782, the British had offered independence to the Americans but, because the offer did not recognize American independence as the negotiations were going on, Jay rejected the offer and brought a stop to the process. The negotiations did not begin again until the fall.

Both Jay and Adams were cornerstones of the American quest for independence and Franklin was a celebrity in Europe. Of the three, Franklin had the most experience as a diplomat and Jay, recognizing his countrymen's standing in the delicate chess match of negotiations, sought lodgings near those of Franklin so that he could learn from the wily, engaging Philadelphian.

There was some friction among the three negotiators; John Adams was not enamored of Franklin and felt that he was past his prime. Jay and Adams did not share Franklin's confidence that the French would deal honorably with the negotiations. This dissension would actually benefit the Americans as they haggled over terms. But Adams, despite his views, could give credit where it was due, saying of Jay that his influence in the negotiations had made him more important than the rest of the Americans on the committee.

Finally, the proposed terms were to the Americans' liking. As John Adams put it, the treaty had secured "the Cod and Ducks and Beavers" for the United States. The

U.S. obtained Newfoundland fishing rights, and the British did acknowledge American independence; in exchange, the Americans were to stop seizing Loyalist property. The treaty did not solve all the problems, and by 1812 the two countries would be at war again, but Jay's role in the negotiations marked him as a man skilled in the art of diplomacy.

On September 3, 1783, the Treaty of Paris was signed. It was ratified by the American Congress of the Confederation on January 14 of the following year, and by Parliament in Great Britain on April 9.

While Jay was in Paris, his father died, leaving Jay with the responsibility of caring for the brother and sister who had been left blind by smallpox when they were children. Jay had other familial responsibilities as well; his brother Frederick was frequently in debt, and his brother Augustus suffered from mental illness. For both brothers, Jay's financial resources and emotional support added to his cares. He had endured family turmoil as a result of his politics as well; his brother James had been a member of the New York State Senate as a representative of the Loyalists, opposed to his brother John's views. Jay, like many of his colleagues, found that the great and weighty matters of state did not come to a halt as personal issues came to the fore.

But the Treaty of Paris was concluded, and the war had ended. His international work accomplished, Jay was once again in service to his country and back on American soil. Upon his return in 1784, he discovered that Congress had elected him to the position of Secretary of Foreign Affairs, a position he would hold until 1789.

Once again, his work brought him into contact with the Spanish government. He made the request of Congress to surrender American claims to the free navigation of the Mississippi River, which was controlled by the Spanish who were in possession of New Orleans. In exchange, Jay wanted to negotiate a beneficial treaty for trade and commerce. His request alarmed the southern states and pointed out the fragility of the internal government and the stability of the country. No one could see in the eighteenth century that it would take a terrible and decimating war in the nineteenth century to resolve those differences which were surfacing.

Jay felt that his mission was to develop a solid, enduring foreign policy, knowing that the long-established nations of Europe could prey upon the United States if its leaders were not vigilant and alert. He pursued recognition of the country by the governments of Europe so that the country could form alliances to its benefit. He sought to build a stable currency, by obtaining loans from European banks. Paying off the war debt that the U.S. had incurred was a priority so that the nation's creditors could be paid back.

In the eyes of the European powers, the New World remained a golden opportunity to advance their territories; knowing this, Jay sought beneficial terms in order to define the boundaries of the United States so that the French, British, and Spanish, and the native tribes as well, could not encroach.

Trade was vital, and Jay sought healthy trade agreements for the goods that American had to offer. As part of trade in international waters, America needed to be safe from pirates.

If American could not solidify the colonies into a nation, no amount of negotiating with foreign powers could help. Building a country was not a matter which could be accomplished only by external means. The former colonies were still sometimes adversarial in their border disputes with their neighbors. Jay and the other Founding Fathers realized that in order to build its strength, America needed to resolve its internal differences. There was no template for the neophyte nation on how to establish itself, and the leaders of the country were left to improvise. They had been forged by war into a collective unit of stable, discerning leaders who believed in the ideals of the new nation. If America was to survive, it needed to be governed with strength. The country was operating under the Articles of Confederation, but as time passed, it became obvious that the Articles failed to allow for sufficient strength in the central government. Something more was needed.

Chapter Five

The Federalist Papers

"If men were angels, no government would be necessary. If angels were to govern men, neither external nor internal controls on government would be necessary. In framing a government which is to be administered by men over men, the great difficulty lies in this: you must first enable the government to control the governed; and in the next place oblige it to control itself."

—James Madison

The American Revolution achieved its goal of winning independence from Great Britain. But the colonies had been English subjects since the early sixteenth century and independence would require a different way of thinking about their responsibilities as citizens of a country which was unlike any other. Not all of the nascent Americans were in accord about what kind of government to create; some Americans still could not conceive of a nation which was not ruled by a king.

The war between the British and the Americans officially ended in 1783 with the signing of the Treaty of Paris. During that time, the country had been governed by the Articles of Confederation. John Jay realized, as did many other of the American leaders, that the Articles of

Confederation failed to address the need for a government that had centralized power and could govern over the individual states. Jay noted that "The Congress under the Articles of Confederation may make war, but are not empowered to raise men or money to carry it on—they may make peace, but without power to see the terms of it observed—they may form alliances, but without ability to comply with the stipulations on their part—they may enter into treaties of commerce, but without power to [e]nforce them at home or abroad...—In short, they may consult, and deliberate, and recommend, and make requisitions, and they who please may regard them."

It was not surprising that the states regarded their individual interests with more emphasis than they did the interests of the central government. Rhode Island was imposing taxes on the traffic that traveled within it via the post road which connected all of the states. Maryland and Virginia were arguing over the Potomac River. In Boston, merchants and farmers had incurred tax debts from the cost of the war. Inflamed by the seizure of their property in exchange for the unpaid debts, the citizens, led by Daniel Shays who hadn't received payment for his service as a captain during the war, rebelled. Even though Shays and his fellow rebels were individuals and not official representatives of the government, banks were foreclosing on loans from unpaid debts.

Massachusetts finally quelled the uprising after some months, but leaders recognized that this was a crisis which would have benefitted from the existence of a federal army capable of bringing a stop to the rebellion. Fearful of the danger of mob rule, the leaders realized that they had to find a solution.

Delegates from five states in attendance at the Annapolis Convention called for a Constitutional Convention to devise a way to improve the Articles of Confederation. The Founding Fathers had defined the problem; now they needed a way to solve it. That gathering began on May 14, 1787, four years after the end of the war, in Philadelphia. Jay was not a member of the Constitutional Convention. Alexander Hamilton was present at the convention for some of the debate, but not on a daily basis, opting to appear periodically in order to express his support for a particular facet of the Constitution. But Virginia's James Madison earned the respect of the other delegates for his leadership, speaking more than 200 times during the debate.

Their task was not a simple one. Their objective was to create a system of government which avoided the flaws inherent in the Articles of Confederation and was strong enough to govern the collective states while being fair enough to allow each state its rights. The federal government was to have three equal branches consisting of an executive, legislative, and judicial arm, all under the power of a system of checks and balances to prevent any single branch from having more power than the other two. The federal government needed to be able to levy taxes, regulate commerce between the states, and devise a means of creating new states out of the vast territories to the west. Another issue which had to be resolved was the question of how to pay the nation's debts incurred during the war.

It was a hot summer in the city, but in order to keep the proceedings concealed from the public, the windows of the meeting hall where the delegates met were nailed shut.

One decision was easily unanimous: George Washington was elected the president of the Constitutional Convention. The leaders recognized the need to define the structure of the government and to list the powers that it would wield. The Constitution needed to be flexible enough to change as circumstances warranted; therefore, there had to be a mechanism by which amendments could be added that reflected the will of the people.

Uniform approval of the finished document was unlikely. Ultimately, of the original 55 delegates, 39 signed the document. Benjamin Franklin explained the dilemma, but as he put it, there really was no dilemma at all. "I doubt too whether any other Convention we can obtain, may be able to make a better Constitution . . . It therefore astonishes me, Sir, to find this system approaching so near to perfection as it does; and I think it will astonish our enemies."

The signatures of the delegates represented one hurdle that was overcome. Obtaining ratification from the American citizens was the next obstacle. Nine of the thirteen states needed to ratify the Constitution for it to become the law of the land. The proponents took to the newspapers to make their case, addressing the objections of those who opposed the document. Some were wary of a central government whose strength would overpower the rights of the individual states.

John Jay, Alexander Hamilton, and James Madison were firmly committed to the success of the Constitution, and they put their pens to the argument in favor of its ratification. They presented their arguments in a series of 85 articles known as *The Federalist Papers* to persuade the members of the New York State convention to ratify the proposed Constitution of the United States.

The trio wrote under the name of Publius; Jay was the author of the second, third, fourth, fifth, and sixty-fourth articles, which focused on the dangers posed by foreign influences. In his *Address to the People of the State of New York on the Subject of the Federal Constitution* , Jay made his case that the Articles of Confederation were ineffective. Had he not been injured during the Doctors' Riot in 1788 during his efforts to soothe an angry mob that was outraged by the body-snatching that was taking place in local New York graveyards, Jay might have contributed more articles to *The Federalist Papers*.

The Federalist Papers made the argument that if the nation did not have a strong central government, the states would no longer be united as a single nation which could take its place among the powers of the world. The Congress would be representative of the states. Thanks to the system of checks and balances, power would be equally divided.

Although *The Federalist Papers* probably didn't weigh heavily upon the minds of the citizens, the essays were considered worthy of being published in the form of a book in 1788. The viewpoints of John Jay, Alexander Hamilton, and James Madison are regarded by historians as a significant and coherent interpretation of the principles upon which the United States is governed according to the Constitution.

New York ratified the Constitution on July 26, 1788, the 11th state to do so. But it was New Hampshire, the ninth state to ratify, which made the Constitution the governing document of the United States of America. The new nation had a government, one comprised of three equal sections. John Jay, who had been instrumental in the forging of the country, was about to inaugurate one of those three branches.

Chapter Six

Chief Justice of the Supreme Court

"Justice is indiscriminately due to all, without regard to wealth, numbers, or rank."

—John Jay

George Washington took the oath of office on April 30, 1789, to become the first president of the United States of America. With the ratification of the Constitution in 1788, the United States had its foundation and the president had his mandate. He also had a role in mind for John Jay, especially after Jay declined to accept the newly-formed position of Secretary of State, which was the former Secretary of Foreign Affairs.

The Chief Justice of the Supreme Court was destined to be, in Washington's view, "the keystone of our political fabric." On September 26, 1789, John Jay was unanimously confirmed by the Senate; the associate justices were John Rutledge, William Cushing, James Wilson, John Blair, Jr., and James Iredell. In this role, Jay was on untrodden ground and began by establishing procedures under which the Supreme Court would function.

The Judiciary Act of 1789 was the first bill to be introduced into the United States Senate. The country was divided into 13 judicial districts. Each district was organized into an eastern, middle, and southern circuit. The justices were require to hold circuit court twice a year in each of the judicial districts.

The Supreme Court was scheduled to gather on February 1, 1790, in New York City, which was at that time the capital of the United States. However, transportation was a challenge in the early days of the nation and not all of the justices could be present, forcing Jay to reschedule the first meeting for February 2.

During Jay's term as chief justice, the Supreme Court heard only four cases, the first one, *West v. Barnes*, in the Court's third term, on August 2, 1791.

William West, a Rhode Island militia general during the American Revolution, had paid the mortgage on his farm for 20 years. In 1785, he asked Rhode Island for permission to set up and run a lottery so that he could pay off the remainder of his mortgage. Recognizing his war service, the state agreed. Proceeds were mostly paid in paper currency rather than in silver or gold. West made his payment in paper currency.

Attorney David Leonard Barnes brought a lawsuit asserting that the payment needed to be made in gold or silver, not paper. West represented himself in the circuit court in 1791, and his argument was rejected; he appealed to the Supreme Court on a writ of error, but could not make the journey to represent himself, instead hiring the Attorney General of Pennsylvania to represent him.

Barnes noted that the writ had not been signed by the Supreme Court clerk. West lost his farm, and the Supreme Court decreed that a writ of error must be issued by the Supreme Court clerk, and not a lower court clerk, within ten days. Based upon the result, Congress modified the procedure so that citizens who lived a distance from the capital could obtain a writ from the circuit court.

The next case came to the Supreme Court in 1792. The Supreme Court was asked to determine whether Congress could assign certain non-judicial duties to the federal circuit courts. The issue involved the Invalid Pensions Act of 1792, regarding pensions for veterans of the American Revolution and in Jay's view, this was not a judicial function. Although the Court did not rule on *Hayburn's Case*, it had come before the Circuit Courts of New York, North Carolina, and Pennsylvania, before five of the six members of the Supreme Court, who declared it unconstitutional. The Supreme Court declined to rule on the lower court decision, despite the appeal by Edmund Randolph, who was the Attorney General of the United States. The issue was eventually resolved after Congress reassigned the disputed duties, and the Supreme Court did not issue a judgment.

The Supreme Court's third case was also the most important case to come during Jay's term as chief justice. *Chisholm v. Georgia* came before the Court in 1793 to settle the question of whether Georgia was subject to the jurisdiction of the federal government and the Supreme Court. Land belonging to two South Carolina Loyalists had been seized by Georgia. The Supreme Court, ruling 4-

1, ruled in favor of the Loyalists, basing its decision upon the view that the states were subject to the process of judicial review. When Georgia made the claim that the federal courts did not have authority over the state, the Supreme Court said that interstate conflicts fell under the authority of the federal government. Jay also described Georgia as an artificial being, a description which stirred the ire of the strong states' rights faction. Jay's opinion was that the people are the sovereign of the United States and that in a lawsuit of this nature, Georgia was not a sovereign.

This was the first Court decision to be overturned by an amendment to the Constitution; the addition of the Eleventh Amendment denied the Supreme Court the right to give a ruling on a case in which a state was being sued by a citizen who belonged to another state or country. It was also the first case in which judicial review was introduced.

The fourth case of Jay's term once again featured the state of Georgia. Jay's Court ruled in *Georgia v. Brailsford* that jurors had the right to "determine the law as well as the fact in controversy." Jay explained that on questions of law, it was the province of the court to decide, but on questions of fact, it was up to the jury to decide; ultimately, both law and facts fell within the jury's power of decision.

Jay began the precedent enforcing the independence of the court. Alexander Hamilton, who was Secretary of the Treasury, asked Chief Justice Jay to endorse legislation assuming the states' debts. Jay declined to take a stance on the issue.

Being a Supreme Court justice was hardly a glamorous position. Having to ride the circuit to hear cases during a time when travel was excruciatingly primitive was a burden. The Court's first justices keenly felt the limited stature and power of the Court, and Jay felt that the role of the Supreme Court was to decide between two litigants in order to determine which case was correct in legal terms. He did not feel that it was the Court's position to become involved in decisions which involved the constitutionality of federal law.

At that time, Supreme Court justices were not forbidden from becoming involved in political matters, a license which allowed Jay to ride the circuit to publicize President Washington's decision to remain neutral in the war between France and Great Britain. President Washington called upon Jay to travel abroad to negotiate a treaty with Great Britain to address unresolved issues between the two countries; the treaty would make Jay extremely unpopular in political circles and would also affect his political hopes. Jay had other political aspirations and had not abandoned hopes of national office. In the 1796 election, he won five electoral votes. The election went to John Adams. He ran again in 1800, and only won one vote.

In 1795, John Jay resigned from the Court. He would not reconsider in 1800 when President John Adams begged him to return as chief justice; he gave his wife's poor health as the reason for his refusal, but Jay also felt that the Court lacked "energy, weight and dignity."

Chapter Seven

The Unpopular Jay Treaty

"John Jay, ah! the arch traitor—seize him, drown him, burn him, flay him alive."

—Newspaper editor

As the United States of America continued its experiment in representative government, the world around it was functioning as it had been doing for centuries. Although Great Britain had signed the peace treaty in Paris granting its former colonies their independence, the British were not pacified. If the infant nation wanted to take its place on the world stage, it was going to have to learn that the big boys played tough.

In 1794, there was friction between the world's two English-speaking nations. Great Britain had blocked the entrance of America's exports with tariffs and trade restrictions, yet English products dominated the markets of the 13 states. The forts which, by terms of the Treaty of Paris, Great Britain had agreed to surrender, were still occupied in the north. Great Britain had seized hundreds of American merchant vessels that were carrying contraband from the French West Indies. To serve its mighty fleet, Great Britain was impressing American sailors and seizing supplies that were on their way to the ports of British enemies, although the United States was neutral in the conflict.

President Washington, who saw his young nation as one which could easily be demolished if it were to be caught up in the web of competing conflicts which had turned the continent of Europe into an endlessly bleeding battlefield, opposed James Madison's desire to fight a trade war. Madison was convinced that the war with France had debilitated Great Britain to the point that the British would automatically concede terms to the Americans without entering a state of war. Washington, ever wary of foreign entanglements, disagreed and instructed Alexander Hamilton to send Chief Justice Jay to Great Britain as a special envoy to negotiate a new treaty and to provide guidelines for the details of the negotiations.

Jay returned from abroad in March 1795 with what was called the Jay Treaty. The British granted "most favoured nation" status to the Americans and agreed to surrender control of the northwestern posts. The United States agreed that it would have restricted access to trade in the British West Indies. But because Hamilton had disclosed to the British that the United States would not join Sweden and Denmark in defending their neutral status, Jay was denied the bargaining leverage that he needed.

For opponents of Washington's foreign policy, the reaction was outrage. The result of this fissure led to the emergence of two separate, competing political parties during Washington's tenure, something that he had hoped would not take place. But the divergent policies of the Federalist and the Democratic-Republican parties would not allow for mediation or compromise.

The southern states felt betrayed because Jay's Treaty did not achieve compensation for the slaves they had lost to the British during the American Revolution. Dedicated supporters of republicanism like Madison and Jefferson feared that strong bonds of trade with the British would weaken American democracy.

Hamilton and his Federalists were not without their support, and they mounted a fierce campaign in favor of the treaty. Washington had political capital, and he used it to support ratification of the treaty. His efforts were successful and the Senate, meeting the requirement for a two-thirds majority, ratified the Jay Treaty by a vote of 20-10.

Jay was vilified for his role in negotiating the hated treaty. He made the joke that it would have been possible for him to travel by night from Boston to Philadelphia with only the burning effigies of his image to light the way.

What the opponents of the treaty failed to recognize was that Jay's Treaty bought much-needed time for a nation that was not equipped yet to take on the mighty British Empire for a second round of war. That war would come in 1812 when the United States had better established itself among the nations as an independent entity, but in 1794, such was not the case.

Jay had national political ambitions and sought the presidency, but the part he played in the Jay Treaty cast him in the light of one who was conciliatory to British interests. He was also known to be an abolitionist, and this trait did not endear him to the slave owners in upstate New York's Dutch region.

Jay turned his attention to his home state and was elected governor of New York in 1795. He had previously run for office in 1792 as the Federalist candidate, but Democratic-Republican candidate George Clinton defeated him, although Jay garnered more votes. According to the New York State Constitution, the cast votes had to be delivered to the secretary of state by the sheriff or his deputy. At the time of the election, the term for the Otsego County sheriffs had expired and the office was vacant, preventing the votes from being delivered according to specification to the New York State capital. Clinton advocates refused to acknowledge the argument that by not delivering the votes from the county, the constitutional rights of the citizens in that county were being violated. The votes were disqualified, and George Clinton won the governorship of the state.

Upon returning to the United States following his time in Great Britain, Jay learned that, during his absence, he had been elected to the governorship of New York. He concentrated his attention on New York and was elected to a second term in 1798. His achievements included reform measures in the areas of prisons and justice as well as construction, particularly of roads and canals.

While he was serving as governor, fellow New Yorker Alexander Hamilton sent him a proposal to gerrymander their state for the upcoming presidential election. Jay did not reply to the request, but on the letter, he wrote, "proposing a measure for party purposes which it would not become me to adopt."

Perhaps Jay's most significant reform was in the abolition of slavery. Jay had been a slave owner, as were many Americans, including northerners. But just as his views on independence had evolved, so did his views on the abolition of slavery. In 1798, Jay owned eight slaves. In 1799, the New York state legislature passed a law endorsing gradual emancipation of all the slaves in New York. By the time of Jay's death in 1829, slavery had been abolished in his home state.

Chapter Eight

Retirement

"That men should pray and fight for their own freedom, and yet keep others in slavery, is certainly acting a very inconsistent, as well as unjust and, perhaps, impious part, but the history of mankind is filled with instances of human improprieties."

—John Jay

His term as governor ended, Jay did not wish to run for another term, and after he declined the nomination to become Chief Justice of the Supreme Court again, Jay retired to be a farmer in Westchester Counter in 1801. He had inherited land from his grandparents and built Bedford House there, near Katonah, New York. It was to this place that the Jays retired after leaving politics.

Years before, in 1776, when his labor on behalf of the nation necessitated frequent separation from his wife, he wrote, "a kind of Confidence or Pre Sentiment that we shall yet enjoy many good Days together, and I indulge myself in imaginary Scenes of Happiness which I expect in a few Years to be realized. If it be a Delusion, it is a pleasing one, and therefore I embrace it. Should it like a Bubble vanish into Air, Resignation will blunt the Edge of

Disappointment, and a firm Persuasion of after Bliss give me Consolation."

Those hopes were not to be. Not long after Jay retired, his wife died. In 1807, Jay had the remains of his wife and his family members moved from the Manhattan family vault to Rye, where he had grown up. Despite the fact that the union between Jay and his wife lacks the fame of the bond between John and Abigail Adams, historian Joseph Ellis, who has reviewed Jay's papers as resources for his writing, notes that the letters exchanged between the two are equal to the correspondence of the Adamses. "There's a level of candor and intimacy and sharing of private thoughts that most 18th-century marriages didn't have."

In 1813, Jay inherited his childhood home in Rye, New York after the death of his older brother, Peter; that property was given to Peter Augustus Jay, the oldest son, in 1822.

His political life was over, and there was a new generation of political leaders as the Founding Fathers receded into the background. But some of the problems with which the Founding Fathers had grappled but had been unable to solve were resurfacing with a vigor that boded ill for the country. Slavery, of course, was perhaps the most severe of the divisions. Although Jay was out of the limelight, his commitment to the abolition of slavery was greater than his political identity, and in 1819, as Missouri was bidding for statehood, Jay wrote a letter condemning its entry as a slave state. He wrote that slavery "ought not to be introduced nor permitted in any of the new states."

Jay had not always been an abolitionist. In his earlier days he, like many other well-to-do New Yorkers, owned slaves. There is irony in the fact that colonists, when making their case against the unfair treatment of the British, protested that Great Britain was treating the colonists as if they were slaves. But in 1777, Jay had changed his position on slavery and drafted a law to abolish slavery in New York. The measure failed the first time, and then a second time when it was introduced in 1785. At issue was the dilemma of what to do with slaves once they were freed.

Jay's commitment to abolition led him to found the New York Manumission Society in 1785. The society coordinated boycotts against merchants involved in the slave trade and offered legal assistance for those freed slaves who were kidnapped in an attempt to force them back into servitude. Jay called upon the support of the New York Manumission Society when he was governor to pass the law calling for the gradual emancipation of New York's slaves. According to the law, *An Act for the Gradual Abolition of Slavery*, all children born from July 4, 1799, to parents who were slaves would be freed, and the exporting of slaves would be forbidden. The law required the children to serve as indentured servants to the person who owned their mothers. Owners would not be compensated for the loss of their slaves. It was not a perfect solution to the issue. But by 1827, all slaves in New York were emancipated in what was possibly the greatest emancipation event to take place on the continent of North America between 1783-1861. The next emancipation would come about as a result of the Civil War and President Abraham Lincoln's Emancipation Proclamation.

One of Jay's methods of fighting against slavery was to buy them and then give them their freedom as adults. However, this was in part altruism, and in part, a business transaction, as he gave them their freedom when he felt that they had provided sufficient work in exchange for the price he had paid.

John Jay spent his retirement in caring for his farm, continuing his efforts for the abolition of slavery, and serving as president of the American Bible Society.

On May 14, 1829, John Jay suffered a stroke. He remained alive for three days before dying on May 17. He had stipulated that instead of giving him an expensive funeral, his family was instead to donate $200 to a poor widow or an orphan. He was buried in the cemetery that he had established in Rye, which is now the oldest active cemetery associated with a person who was part of the American Revolution. The private cemetery is maintained by the descendants of John Jay.

How has history assessed this modest Founding Father, the one who seems to have been forgotten? Even historian Joseph Ellis admits that when he wrote his book *Founding Brothers*, he neglected to include Jay among the chief architects of the United States, an omission he rectified in his later work, *The Quartet*. Ellis credits four men—George Washington, James Madison, Alexander Hamilton, and John Jay—with the achievement of turning the United States from a confederation of former colonies into a nation. He believes that, if he is correct in his assertion, "this was arguably the most creative and consequential act of political leadership in American history."

One of the reasons that Jay has been so unrecognized as other Founding Fathers have been celebrated in media ranging from serious scholarly works to popular culture is that his papers were not available. Columbia University Professor Richard Morris had control of the Jay papers and documents, but it was only after the death of Morris that the papers have been made available in the past decade.

Jay's influence touched every sphere of contact for the new nation. He supported independence and fought a covert war as a spymaster against the enemies of the Americans, attended the Continental Congresses, negotiated international treaties, served as the first Supreme Court Justice, and became the governor of his home state of New York. He was the equal of the other Founding Fathers in his accomplishments and attributes. Perhaps, in his humility, he was their superior.

Made in the USA
Lexington, KY
11 May 2019